The Golden Retriever

by Mary Casanova

Edited by Julie Bach

CRESTWOOD HOUSE

New York
Collier Macmillan Canada
Toronto
Maxwell Macmillan International Publishing Group
New York   Oxford   Singapore   Sydney

LIBRARY OF CONGRESS CATALOGING-IN-PUBLICATION DATA

Casanova, Mary.
    The golden retriever / by Mary Casanova ; edited by Julie Bach.
  - 1st ed.
      p.   cm. — (Top dog series)
    Summary: Discusses the history, physical characteristics, care,
and breeding of the golden retriever.
     ISBN 0-89686-525-8
     1. Golden retrievers—Juvenile literature. [1. Golden
retrievers. 2. Dogs.] I. Bach, Julie S., 1963- . II. Title.
III. Series: Top dog (Crestwood House)
SF429.G63C37   1990
636.7'52—dc20

90-34141
CIP
AC

PHOTO CREDITS
Cover: Elizabeth Fox / Gracie owned by Rebecca Tachna
Kent and Donna Dannen: 4, 31, 42
Elizabeth Fox: 7, 14, 17, 28, 32
Mary Ellen Casey: 9
Leslie Dickerson: 12
Cindy Lichtenberger: 19, 22, 25, 37, 40

CRESTWOOD HOUSE

Macmillan Publishing Company
866 Third Avenue
New York, NY 10022

Collier Macmillan Canada, Inc.
1200 Eglinton Avenue East
Suite 200
Don Mills, Ontario M3C 3N1

Printed in the United States of America
First Edition
10 9 8 7 6 5 4 3 2 1

◤CONTENTS

For more information about golden retrievers, write to:

American Kennel Club
51 Madison Avenue
New York, NY 10010

Golden Retriever Club of America*
Kathy Heisler
21640 Thirty Mile Road
Romeo, MI 48065

*This address will change as new officers are selected. The current
address is always available from the AKC.

AS GOOD AS GOLD

Walk in the park. A large amber dog is romping with children. Go to a dog show. A handsome golden is winning the blue ribbon. Drive through the countryside. A team of goldens helps a hunter bring in wildfowl from the fields. Stroll through the city. A trustworthy golden leads a blind woman across the street. Turn on the news. Police dogs sniff out illegal drugs, and golden retrievers are part of the team.

Why is the golden retriever so popular? The answer is easy. The golden retriever, or golden, as it is often called, is a talented dog with a big heart. It is sturdy and quick—a strong swimmer and good tracker. It can withstand foul weather and icy waters. It's intelligent enough to learn anything—the skills of a guide dog, police dog, or show dog. And it's gentle enough to be part of a family.

The golden retriever likes people, all people. It might bark at an intruder, but it'll be wagging its tail at the same time. The golden is a friend to everyone.

As a family dog, the golden retriever is

A good tracker and a good friend, the golden retriever has become a favorite with hunters and pet owners alike.

second to none. Patient and good-natured, the golden retriever is famous for its gentle disposition. It'll let toddlers crawl over it unharmed. And it won't play too roughly with older kids. It's loyal and faithful. It's unlikely that you'll find a golden retriever wandering far from home. Content to be near you, it will stay at your side or at your feet.

As a hunting dog, show dog, and family dog, the golden retriever is as good as gold.

A GOLDEN HISTORY

Where does the golden retriever *breed* come from? Let's look back in time. Scientists trace all pet dogs back to a form of wild dog or wolf.

Evidence indicates that dogs first became *domesticated* about 12,000 years ago. People probably tamed the wild dogs to help them hunt. About 6,000 years ago in ancient Egypt, artists carved pictures in stone of dogs with their owners. Over time, people bred dogs with physical and behavior traits they liked best.

Goldens were once believed to have come from Russia. But the breed we know today came from the fields and woodlands of Scotland and England. In the early part of the 19th century, the sport of hunting with guns became popular. Hunters shot wildfowl and needed capable dogs to retrieve their game.

Dogs with sharp retrieving and tracking skills were bred to hunt in fields and in the water. Owners crossed setters and spaniels with a lightly built Newfoundland breed from the British coast. Unlike today's Newfoundland, it was noted for its swimming and retrieving skills and its endurance.

Lively and active dogs, goldens love to run on beaches and swim.

This *breeding* led to four retriever breeds—the curly coat, the wavy or flat coat, the Labrador, and the golden, or yellow, as it was then called.

The father of the golden line of retrievers came from a litter of wavy coats owned by an English cobbler. All of the puppies were black except one: an odd, yellow, wavy-coated pup named Nous. The cobbler needed to settle his debts. He sold the pup to Lord Chichester in 1865, who then sold it to Lord Tweedmouth.

Lord Tweedmouth, an Englishman, lived on an estate in Scotland. There he spent much of his time hunting. His love of hunting led him on a quest for the perfect hunting dog.

Lord Tweedmouth saw great potential in Nous, the yellow puppy. Nous became the father of a famous bloodline called Guisachan, the foundation for the golden retriever breed.

In 1909, eight golden retrievers were entered in a dog show in London. Two years later, the Kennel Club of England recognized the dog as a separate breed. For a while, the club called the breed "yellows, or golden retrievers." But in 1920, the name "yellow" was dropped altogether.

The Golden Retriever Club of America (GRCA) reports that the breed started in the

The American Kennel Club officially recognized the golden retriever as a separate breed in 1932.

United States as early as the 1890s. American interest wasn't strong, though, until the early 1930s.

The American Kennel Club (AKC) recognized the golden retriever as a separate breed in 1932. During the same year, a golden named Speedwell Pluto won "Best in Show" and became the first American champion of the breed.

THE GOLDEN RETRIEVER IN CLOSE-UP

As gentle as they are, it's easy to forget that golden retrievers are members of the scientific order *Carnivora,* or meat-eating mammals. Their closest relatives are wolves, foxes, and jackals—all from the family *Canidae.* Scientists refer to all domesticated dogs by the same species name: *Canis familiaris.*

The golden retriever is a separate breed with distinct qualities. When a golden competes in a dog show, it must meet certain standards of its breed to win. These breed standards are set by the AKC and the GRCA to maintain the special qualities of the breed.

The golden male is larger than the female. He measures 23 to 24 inches at the *withers.* He weighs between 67 and 75 pounds. The female, or *bitch,* is 21½ to 22½ inches high. She weighs between 55 and 65 pounds.

The golden's face and eyes have a kindly, intelligent look. The head is broadly shaped with a straight muzzle. The teeth should have a scissors bite, not an underbite or an overbite. Its nose should be black or dark brown. The ears, medium length with rounded edges, hang just below eye level.

The neck and body of the golden retriever are muscular and sturdy. The neck has a *ruff*, or fringe of long hair. The body is well balanced. This means the golden is neither too short nor too long. Its chest is not barrel-shaped, but is deep and well developed. Its back is slightly sloping, flat from the top of the shoulders to the top of the *hindquarters*.

The *forequarters* and hindquarters should be muscular and coordinated. From the front, the dog's legs should appear straight. From the side, the hindquarters will appear bent.

The dog's feet are rounded, like cats' paws, but bigger, of course. They're medium sized with sturdy, thick pads. These pads cushion its feet when the dog is crossing rugged terrain.

A dog's tail indicates how the animal is feeling. Well-cared-for golden retrievers are almost always wagging their tails. When they run, their tails curve up slightly. If they're not feeling well or they lack confidence, their tails hang down between their legs.

When their coats glisten in the sunlight, goldens seem to be bred only for their good

looks. Their coats, however, are both beautiful and functional. They repel icy water and insulate the dogs from biting winds.

The golden retriever's *gait* is smooth and powerful. It's as if the golden glides along without any effort at all. When you watch goldens in action, you'll agree—these dogs are perfectly put together.

THE GOLDEN RETRIEVER'S KEEN SENSES

Dogs, like people, rely on their five senses—smell, hearing, taste, touch, and sight. Unlike humans, dogs rely less on their sense of sight and more on their senses of smell and hearing. Some people say dogs have another sense, an inner sense of navigation, which helps them return home even from many miles away.

Experts say that a golden retriever's sense of smell is a million times better than a human's! It is an important ability. Over the ages, it has helped dogs locate food, mates, and territories.

Its sharp sense of smell enables the golden retriever to find game in fields of long grass.

Golden retrievers are friendly, curious dogs that enjoy playing with other dogs.

A dog's *olfactory system* for smelling is 40 times larger than a human's. This highly developed system means it can smell things you will never smell. A golden can smell a downed bird, for instance, from 40 to 50 yards away. When trained, it can sniff out illegal drugs or dangerous explosives.

A golden's sense of hearing is also amazing. A dog can hear the high pitch of a dog whistle when humans cannot. This sense, too, makes a golden a good hunting dog.

A golden's vision is not as good as a human's, however. It can see better from side to side, but in general, its vision is not as clear. The dog sees poorly close up, and it is color-blind. What a person sees as bright colors, the golden sees as fuzzy shadows. A golden's night vision and long-range vision, however, are better than a human's.

The sense of touch in a golden retriever is not very keen. But this is not a weakness. In a hunting dog, it's a strength. It means the golden can tolerate bitter temperatures without feeling uncomfortable.

THE FRIENDLIEST BREED IN THE WORLD

Gentle, warmhearted, obedient—the golden retriever is everyone's friend. It has a naturally good *temperament*. It's trustworthy, reliable, and easy to train.

A golden retriever is unbeatable with

children. Many small dogs get nervous around children because they're afraid of getting hurt. The golden, however, is easygoing and controlled. It doesn't mind if a toddler crawls over it while it naps.

If you're looking for a ferocious watchdog, don't get a golden retriever. Interested in protecting its home, a golden will usually bark when a stranger comes to the door, but it will wag its tail only a few moments later. It would rather get acquainted than start a fight.

Because of its sociable nature, a golden retriever doesn't do well if left alone often. It needs human contact. If a golden retriever must be outside or in a kennel, it's important to make extra efforts to spend time with it. Shunned from the family, the dog will feel lonely and frustrated. This, in turn, may lead to bad habits, such as chewing, digging, or barking. Avoid these problems. Let the dog visit in the house when everyone is home. Better yet, let it sleep next to your bed.

Perhaps more than any other breed, the golden retriever is by nature obedient. It is eager to learn as much as you're willing to teach it. According to AKC records, golden retrievers have won more obedience titles than any other breed.

Goldens are intelligent, too. They learn quickly and remember everything. They win champion titles at dog shows and field trials. And they work as Seeing Eye dogs for the blind and as search dogs for police.

But the beautiful golden does have one problem—it wants to be treated like a person. And why not? A golden retriever is a smart dog with gentle eyes and a loving nature. Treat it as part of the family and it will repay you with years of close companionship.

Goldens do not like to be alone. They need the company of people or other dogs.

CHOOSING A GOLDEN RETRIEVER

Is a golden retriever for you? Too often, dogs are bought on a whim and later taken to humane societies or abandoned. If you're not ready for the commitment, don't buy a golden. Get a goldfish instead. Asking yourself these questions may help you decide whether you are ready:

Do you have the time and space for a golden retriever? Remember, a golden needs companionship. You must be able to spend time with your dog. Bred for work, it also needs daily exercise. If you live in a city, you and your dog will need a nearby park for playing and walking. You will also need a home big enough to share with a large dog.

Are you patient? A puppy requires close supervision, frequent meals, and housebreaking. As it grows, it has to be trained. Training requires hard work, patience, and lots of time.

Are you ready for a long-term commitment? Remember that puppies grow up to become dogs. Golden retrievers can live 12 years or

18

A golden retriever puppy needs a lot of care and attention to grow into a healthy dog.

longer. You must be ready to give your dog a place in your life for many years to come.

Can you afford a golden retriever? Food and other costs can run as high as $50 per month. There will also be *veterinary* bills to pay.

If you're ready to commit time, money, patience, and love, then you're ready to buy a golden retriever. Here are some points to consider in choosing your new pet.

First, do you want an adult dog or a puppy? An older dog will probably already be trained. It won't require as much care as a puppy. You won't have to guess what the older dog will someday look like. Its coat won't change color, whereas a puppy's coat will continue to darken until it's about five years old. If you choose an older dog, make sure you like its temperament. Its behavior is not likely to change.

Do you want a male or female? Both make fine pets. The male may tend to roam and need more exercise. The female may be more contented. Males generally cost less; females can have puppies. If you don't want to breed your female dog, you'll probably have her *spayed.* This operation costs about $100. She may be less active after spaying. You can also make sure your male dog doesn't make another dog pregnant. Your vet can *neuter* him. That operation costs slightly less than spaying.

Are papers important? If you want a quality show dog, you'll want to have its *pedigree*. This is a chart of its ancestry. The greater a dog's show qualities, the more it will cost. An inexpensive puppy is not necessarily a bargain. It may mean that the puppy lacks careful breeding or proper care. A typical golden costs at least $250. Puppies of champions may sell for as much as $1,000 or more.

Where do you find a golden retriever? An adult dog may be found through a newspaper ad. Puppies are usually bought at a pet store or from a breeder. A pet store generally has only one puppy to look at. A breeder has a whole *litter* from which to choose. A breeder can show you the *dam* and *sire*, the puppies' mother and father. That's important because puppies usually grow up to look and behave like their parents. Be sure to ask questions. A serious breeder will be helpful and knowledgeable.

How do you choose the right puppy? First, make sure it's ready to be *weaned*. It must be at least seven weeks old for that. Second, check out its temperament. If the puppy is listless, it may need a nap or have just eaten dinner.

This golden puppy looks as if it's not sure whether it wants to eat or sleep!

Look at it again after an hour. Then watch how it plays with the other puppies. Avoid those that are too aggressive or too shy. Then, calmly extend your hand. Let it warm up to you. A well-adjusted golden puppy will come to you with its tail wagging. It will be eager to be your friend.

Look for signs of good health. The puppy should have bright, clear, friendly eyes. Its eyes and nose should not be runny. It should have a sturdy build and a thick, shiny coat. Patches in the coat could mean mange, ringworm, or eczema. The inside of its ears should be pink and smooth, not red. Its teeth should be white, and its gums should be firm and pink. Check its hearing by snapping your fingers behind it to get its attention. It should respond.

Ask the breeder if the puppy has been *wormed* or given any vaccinations. If so, find out when, what kind, and if more shots are needed. Also, find out if the puppy's parents have been checked for *hip dysplasia*. This is a hip problem that can be passed on to puppies. Large dogs, including goldens, should be checked for it.

Finally, get a written agreement that allows you to have the puppy examined by your veterinarian before the sale is final. An examination will help assure you that you've chosen a healthy golden retriever.

CARING FOR YOUR GOLDEN RETRIEVER

Once home, your golden relies on you to take care of it. Fortunately, that's not hard to do. At about eight weeks of age, your golden retriever will be eating from a dish. Make sure you provide a balanced diet. Some owners prepare meals from scratch. Others buy commercial food sold in cans, bags, or packages. Whatever kind you choose, make sure it is high quality and nutritious.

Feed your dog at the same time and place every day. It appreciates routine. Water and food dishes should be sturdy and washed often. Avoid feeding your golden table scraps, especially chicken, fish, or pork bones. They can get stuck in its throat.

Grooming your golden retriever is easier than you might think. Goldens are "natural" dogs that don't need their tails or ears clipped. You'll be able to groom your dog yourself. Buy a good dog brush and brush its coat in the same direction the hair grows. Brush it an average of 20 to 30 minutes per week. With little effort, your dog will look radiant.

Though a golden's coat is thick and long, it has a great self-cleaning quality. Goldens should be bathed as infrequently as possible. If they're washed too often, their skin will lose its natural oils and become too dry. Bathe your dog only when you can't clean it any other way. Use a special dog soap and lukewarm water. Towel dry it. If the weather is cold, keep your dog inside until its coat is dry so it doesn't get chilled.

If your dog runs through fields and woods, its coat may become tangled with burrs. Do your best to remove them right away. If you can't pull them out, gently cut them out. Use scissors with rounded points. Your dog's hair will grow back, and it'll feel more comfortable.

The toenails of a golden can grow too long if it doesn't run on gravel or pavement. They can lame a dog if not cut. A vet can trim your dog's nails. Or you can learn how to do it yourself.

A golden has a kind of "self cleaning" coat, so it needs to be bathed only occasionally. Frequent baths could dry out its skin.

Companionship is part of caring for your golden retriever. Be its friend. Stroke it and give it lots of hugs. Find games to play together. Your dog will be happy chasing a tennis ball or playing tug-of-war with an old rag. (Be careful not to pull anything too hard out of a puppy's fragile teeth.) Play tag. But don't get discouraged if you can't catch your golden. It's fast! Throw a stick, and it'll soon start retrieving it.

At the end of the day, where should it sleep? Because your golden is a family dog, it'll be happiest sleeping indoors. Give it a spot of its own—a large dog basket or pad. When it's a puppy, a cage or sleeping box might work best at night.

When you're away from the house, your golden retriever will be comfortable outside. A doghouse will shelter it from the wind, snow, and rain. If you build a fenced enclosure or run, make it large enough for your dog to exercise. Also, always obey leash laws in your area.

When your golden wags its tail and holds its head high, you can take pride. A well-cared-for dog reflects a loving owner.

KEEPING YOUR GOLDEN RETRIEVER HEALTHY

As a breed, the golden retriever is very healthy. The best way to keep your golden fit is with preventive care. Make sure it gets a proper diet, daily exercise, and regular veterinary checkups.

If your dog can't run in a field all day, set aside regular exercise times. Brisk walks through the park are a good idea. Daily exercise will keep your dog physically and mentally alert.

Your local veterinarian can help you keep your golden retriever healthy. After you buy your puppy, take it to the vet for an initial exam. The vet will want to check if it has worms. A puppy can get worms from fleas, worm eggs, or from its mother. If it has worms, the vet will prescribe the right treatment.

Like you, your puppy needs *vaccinations* to prevent common diseases. You've probably heard of distemper and rabies. There are other

27

dog diseases, too. Your veterinarian will tell you which vaccinations your puppy needs and when to get them. After its first shots, your puppy will need booster shots. And after its first year, your golden will need yearly vaccinations. Keep records of all your puppy's shots.

If your dog should become sick, you'll know, especially if you learn to recognize common symptoms. They are weight loss, exhaustion, poor coat condition, coughing and sneezing, runny nose, repeated vomiting or diarrhea, moaning, or unusual saliva. Call your veterinarian if you notice any of them.

Daily exercise will help keep your golden strong and healthy.

Usually the golden retriever is sturdy. A few disorders, however, are common to the breed. The first is hip dysplasia, a problem with the fit of the hip ball-and-socket joint. This is a problem among large dogs. It can be passed on from parents to puppy, so it helps to check the pedigree before buying. The puppy will not show signs of the disorder until it is at least five months old. (Some puppies have problems with their hips due to overly rapid growth. They often outgrow the problems.) Hip dysplasia can be corrected by surgery, but that is costly.

Eye disorders can also be a problem. *Trichiasis* is when a dog's eyelashes turn inward, touching the eyeball. This may lead to squinting, tearing, or inflamed eyes. *Cataracts* impair vision by clouding the lens of the eye. *Progressive retinal atrophy* (PRA) is an ailment passed on from the parent. This can lead to blindness. Make sure the pedigree is free of PRA. If you notice any changes in your dog's eyes, contact your veterinarian.

"Hot spots" can be a problem with goldens. When the thick coat of hair gets wet, it can trap moisture next to the dog's skin. Warm, wet skin is ripe for fungus growth. A hot spot is a tender, inflamed, moist spot on the dog's skin. Left untreated, the surrounding hair will fall out as the hot spot grows. To prevent this, towel dry your dog after it has been swimming.

It's good to be aware of possible health problems. But don't worry. Most dogs stay healthy. With good care, your dog will likely live a full and healthy life.

TRAINING YOUR GOLDEN RETRIEVER

Training your golden retriever is an easy task. That's because goldens are one of the most naturally obedient and intelligent breeds in the world.

Your golden wants to please you. It will learn as much as you're willing to teach it. Your job is to supply plenty of patience and praise. The dog will soak it right up. When it does something right, stroke it and tell it how wonderful it is. This is called *reinforcement*.

When your dog does something wrong, always scold it with a stern "No." Never hit it or it will become hand-shy. In all training, be consistent. Don't change the rules, or the dog

This young golden in a harness is being trained to "fetch."

will get confused. Your dog will soon know that
you're in charge.

One of the first lessons people teach their
dogs is *housebreaking*. This means teaching it
to relieve itself in a place you've chosen. Before
you bring your puppy into the house, give it
time to relieve itself outside. Then in the home
give it a place for sleeping and eating. Take it
outside right after eating and napping, always
to the same area. Be patient, and don't rush
your puppy.

To teach your puppy basic commands, you'll need a good leash and *choke collar*. But use the choke collar only for training. Otherwise, it could get caught on something and choke your dog.

When you want your dog to come to you, say, "Come." Use a friendly voice. Always praise your dog when it obeys. If you scold it, it may not want to come the next time.

To make your puppy sit, stand in front of it and say, "Sit." You may have to push down on its hindquarters to help it get the idea. Regardless, praise it right away.

After your dog masters the "sit" command, the next step is the "lie down" command. When it's sitting, say, "Lie down." At the same time, pull its front legs out until the dog is lying down. Always praise it.

When the dog is sitting or lying down, use the "stay" command. Say, "Stay." Move a short distance from it. When it starts to move, say "Stay" again, in a firm voice. Then, when you want it to move, say, "Come" or "Up."

When you go for walks, you'll want your dog walking at your side, stopping when you stop. This is called *heeling*. When the dog starts getting ahead of you, pull back on the leash, and say, "Heel." When you stop walking, say

Goldens are easy to train. Learning to obey commands comes naturally to them.

"Heel" again, and push the dog's hindquarters down into a sit position. Before long, it'll be walking at your side.

Don't try to teach all of these lessons to your dog in one day. Go slowly, repeating the same lesson over and over until the dog learns it. Add new lessons slowly.

If your puppy gets lots of training and love, it will be happy and satisfied. Problems like digging, jumping on people, and chewing start when puppies are neglected. Don't let these habits get started. Give your dog a toy of its own to chew. Train it. Most importantly, spend time with it. Your dog will be well behaved before you know it.

RAISING GOLDEN RETRIEVER PUPPIES

What could be better than owning your own golden retriever? Why, raising golden retriever puppies, of course. Before you find a *stud* for the mother-to-be, make sure you have extra space for puppies. Also, plan on at least an extra hour of work per day. It takes time to feed and clean up after a litter of active puppies. But they're worth it!

Give your female a chance to grow up before she becomes a mother. Motherhood is a demanding job. Wait until she's at least 16 months old.

Begin by searching for the right father. Puppies have a good chance of becoming like their parents, so be choosy. Find a breeder with a friendly, handsome stud. Check blood-lines, and be sure his pedigree is free of hip dysplasia and eye disorders. Also, before breeding, bring your *bitch* to a vet to make sure she's in excellent health. Any vaccinations or worming must be done before pregnancy.

When your female is in season, or in *heat*, she is ready to mate. Bring her to the breeder you have chosen. Expect to pay a fee or to give the breeder first pick of the litter. Most likely your dog will become pregnant, and you'll have a short nine weeks to prepare for the arrival of puppies.

During her pregnancy, keep your dog on a high-nutrition diet. As her puppies grow, her appetite will increase. Continue to take her on daily walks, but don't let her get too tired.

Before the puppies are born, you will need to set up a *whelping box.* This is a wooden box where the mother will give birth and care for her young. It must be large enough for the mother to stretch out in and high enough to hold her puppies. Line it with layers of newspaper and an old, washable blanket. Keep the temperature in the whelping box at about 70 to 80 degrees Fahrenheit. You'll know the big day is getting closer when the mother starts getting restless. Give her plenty of peace and quiet as the birth nears.

Most puppies are born in the night. Stay close by the mother's side, speaking softly to her. She'll start panting. When the contractions start, you'll see her sides moving as she starts delivering her puppies. The first puppy will slide out at the *vulva.* With her teeth, the mother will open the birth sac, which encases the puppy. Then she'll shred the *umbilical cord.* To help her puppy start breathing, she'll lick it roughly. Don't get upset if she eats the afterbirth. This is nature's way of helping milk production and keeping the labor going.

A puppy will be born about every half hour. Plan on a long night, as the average litter size for a golden is eight puppies. Though their eyes will be closed, the puppies' keen sense of smell will help them find their mother's *teats,* ready with warm milk.

Golden retriever puppies should be handled gently.

Most likely, all you'll have to do is watch the miracle of birth. But sometimes the mother is unable to finish delivery and needs your help. If so, firmly clamp off the puppy's umbilical cord in the middle and use rounded scissors to cut the cord a few inches from the puppy's navel. Carefully tear the membrane casing from around the puppy. Open its mouth and remove any mucus. Then, briskly rub it with a warm towel for about 15 minutes.

Otherwise, avoid handling the puppies at first. Let the mother care for them herself. The less you handle them, the better. She may want to protect the puppies. Be understanding. Before long, she'll welcome your help.

As the puppies grow, you'll want to cuddle and play with them. They're soft balls of fur that are easy to love. Your gentle handling is important. They'll learn their social skills from you. Playing well with them will make them better pets.

When the puppies near four weeks old, it will be time to begin weaning them. They must go from nursing to eating solid food. Dip your finger in a flat dish of lukewarm puppy food and put some on the puppy's nose. It'll lick it off and start searching for more. Feed your puppies four times a day. Soon, they'll be nursing only at night. By five or six weeks old, they should be completely weaned.

At six to seven weeks, bring the puppies to your veterinarian for their first shots. Your vet will want to check for worms, so bring a few *stool samples*, too.

At seven weeks, it will be time for the puppies to go to new homes. Find them good homes where there is lots of love!

SHOWING YOUR GOLDEN RETRIEVER

Competition is hard work, but it can be fun, too. It's satisfying to win an award or ribbon. For the registered golden retriever, there are three types of competition—bench, field, and obedience.

In bench competition, your dog is judged in the show ring for its appearance. The judges compare it to other goldens and against the breed standard.

Your dog must learn to stand still while it's being judged. The judges will look it over from head to toe. They'll even look in its mouth. Among other things, they'll look for a shiny coat and clear, bright eyes. If your dog is close to perfect, it may win Best of Breed!

Field competition takes you to the fields and lakes. It tests your dog's hunting and retrieving skills. In the marking test, your dog will see a bird go down and then have to go find it. In the blind test, it won't see the bird go down, so it'll have to find it by your signals. To compete, your golden must have strong retrieving skills on both land and water. If you enjoy a challenge, then working toward National Retriever Champion may be for you.

The third type of competition is obedience competition. The *handler* and dog are judged in the ring on how well they work together. The dog must obey the handler's commands. You can train your dog at home, or you may wish to take it to an obedience school. Either way, it'll have to be well behaved to win.

If competition interests you, write to the AKC. They'll send you information about

Judges check each golden retriever's teeth, eyes, and coat before choosing the Best of Breed at a show.

registration, rules, and sporting etiquette. They can also tell you about how to get started in Junior Showmanship, competition for boys and girls 14 years old and under.

Whether in the show ring or on the field, you and your golden retriever will have to work hard. But the work can be fun and very rewarding.

TRAINING YOUR FIELD AND WATER DOG

It's the opening day of hunting season. The air is icy fresh and spiced with the aroma of autumn leaves. Your golden retriever walks at your side, awaiting your signal. You've worked hard together, training for this day. A good hunter, you know that a wounded bird not retrieved is a waste. That's why you and your dog are a team. It follows your commands, at times seeming to read your mind. You shoot. It finds the duck, carries it back in its mouth, and

A favorite pastime of golden retrievers is retrieving! This dog is practicing for a field trial.

drops it at your feet. You stroke your dog's fine head and praise it for its excellent work.

How do you train your dog for field and water retrieving? Start with the basic lessons of obedience training. Gradually, teach your dog to respond to a whistle, too. Use one short whistle for "sit." Use a series of short, sharp whistles for "come."

It's natural for a golden to retrieve. Goldens will go after a stick or *dummy* you've tossed, and bring it back to you. The challenge is in getting the dog to let go of it.

When your puppy is about four or five months old, start simple retrieving lessons. You'll both have fun. Start by throwing a knotted towel. Say, "Fetch." Then, when it brings it to you, say "Give," and lavish your puppy with praise. If it won't let go, press its upper lip over its teeth to get it to open, saying, "Give." Be patient, and never chase your puppy or play tug-of-war during lesson time. To help your dog learn, keep a few treats in your pocket, too.

As your puppy learns to retrieve, start using more dummies so that it will learn to look for more game. Throw the first. When it retrieves it, throw a second dummy, and then a third. These dummies should be thrown in opposite directions. You want your dog to learn to search for more than one bird but to retrieve only one at a time.

A dog is naturally afraid of the sound of guns. You must work with your puppy so that it doesn't become gun-shy. Fire the first shot at least 500 feet away from it. Gradually move closer. After a while, it will learn that the sound of gunshot means a wounded bird, and it'll be ready to investigate.

Water-retrieving lessons should begin in warm weather. Never force your puppy into the water. To help it get the idea, bring an older dog along. Or, put on your swimsuit and jump in. Make it fun. Your dog will soon be jumping in with you. Begin water-retrieving lessons at a later time. When you do, use a commercial dummy or a cork-filled boat bumper—something soft that floats.

To help your dog learn to carry game in its mouth, practice with a dead bird. Experts recommend using a pigeon or a small duck with its wings tied securely to its body. This helps your dog learn to grab the whole bird in its mouth, not just a wing.

If you want further assistance with training, go to a dog training school together, or consult a professional dog trainer. Also, read more about training. Training is hard work, but learning together can be worthwhile and satisfying.

Your day of hunting has come to an end. The sun, low in the sky, paints the horizon shades of mauve and amber. Slung over your shoulder is a game bag full of ducks. At your side strides your faithful hunting partner. You press home, ready to tell of your adventures with the best hunting dog in the world—your own golden retriever.

GLOSSARY/ INDEX

Bitch 10, 35—An adult female dog.

Breed 6, 8, 9, 10, 15, 16, 27, 30, 39—A particular kind of dog with common ancestors and similar characteristics. A golden retriever is one breed of dog.

Breeding 8—Mating a quality female to a quality male.

Cataracts 29—An eye disease that clouds the lens and causes partial or total blindness.

Choke Collar 33—A lead made from heavy metal links. It is used in training a dog.

Dam 21—The mother of a litter of puppies.

Domesticated 6—To be made tame and able to live with people.

Dummy 42, 43—An object that resembles a bird, thrown to teach dogs how to retrieve.

Forequarters 11—A dog's front legs.

Gait 13—The movements of a dog's feet when it is walking, trotting, or running.

Grooming 24—Bathing and brushing a dog to keep its coat clean and smooth.

Handler 40—The person who manages a dog in a show or contest.

Heat 35—The days when a bitch is ready to mate.

Heeling 33, 34—When a dog walks obediently at its owner's side.

Hindquarters 11—A dog's back legs.

Hip Dysplasia 23, 29—A disorder of the hip joint in dogs that is often passed from parent to puppy.

Housebreaking 18, 31—Training a puppy to relieve itself on newspaper or outside the house.

Litter 21, 35, 36—A family of puppies born at a single whelping.

Olfactory System 14—The nerve endings inside the nose that sense odors.

Neuter 20—To remove the testes of a male dog to prevent him from making a female pregnant.

Pedigree 21, 35—A chart that lists a dog's ancestors.

Progressive Retinal Atrophy (PRA) 29—An eye disease, common to some breeds, which slowly leads to blindness.

Reinforcement 30—Giving a dog a reward when it obeys a command.

Ruff 11—A fringe of long hair on a dog's neck.

Sire 21—The father of a litter of puppies.

Spaying 20—Removing a female dog's ovaries to prevent pregnancy.

Stool Sample 38—A sample of a dog's feces used for medical testing.

Stud 34, 35—A purebred male used for breeding.

Teats 36—A female dog's nipples. Puppies suck on the teats to get milk.

Temperament 15—A dog's typical emotional behavior, or way of acting.

Trichiasis 29—An eye disorder that makes eyelashes grow inward.

Umbilical Cord 36, 37—A hollow tube that carries nutrients to a puppy while it is in its mother's body.

Vaccinations 27—Shots given to protect a dog from diseases.

Veterinarian 20, 23, 27, 28, 38—A doctor who is trained to take care of animals.

Vulva 36—The entrance to the birth canal.

Weaning 21, 38—To make a puppy stop drinking its mother's milk and eat solid food instead.

Whelping Box 36—A box in which a female dog can give birth to her puppies.

Withers 10—A dog's shoulders; the point where its neck joins the body. A dog's height is measured at the withers.

Worm 23—To rid a dog of dangerous parasites that live in its intestines.